Pacific Northwest Fishing Journal

Contact me if found

Owner _____

Address _____

_____

_____

Phone (home) _____

Phone (mobile) _____

Email _____

The Pacific Northwest Fishing Journal is designed to document fishing adventures in the ocean and tide influenced rivers and bays.

This journal was made by anglers for anglers. We live and fish in the Pacific Northwest.

Fishing has little to do with luck and a lot to do with experience and skill. It's a science. Over time, memory isn't very reliable. This journal will provide a handy reference of where you fished, what you caught and how you caught it - from week to week and year to year.

This is the only fishing journal that can manage data from fishing multiple species using different methods in varying water systems in a single trip as well as document crab catches. It's how anglers fish in the PNW!

How to use the Pacific Northwest Fishing Journal

The journal includes room for a lot of data. Document the information that is important and relevant to you.

Each fishing trip has two facing pages to add information:

- The left page includes data collected before heading out, such as tides, sunrise and sunset, temperature and barometric pressure.
- Below that are sections specific to the ocean, river/bay and crab pots. Enter information relevant to your trip.
- Notes section – we include river sections or areas we trolled or drifted but got skunked or scored, lures or bait that weren't working, fishing reports, boat issues, and water issues. Basically anything that may hint at why fishing was better or worse than expected.
- The facing page is a table to document your catches. If you have an exceptional day fishing, use an additional table on the following page. We put a "K" next to keepers and "R" for the fish released.

We generally fish out of the same boat and keep this journal in the glove box. The size of this journal is convenient enough to toss in a dry bag for the drift boat.

Date _____ Time Launch _____AM/PM Time Out _____AM/PM

Port/Dock _____

Fishing Buddies _____

High Tide_____ Low Tide _____

Sunrise _____AM Sunset _____PM

Air Temp Range _____ Barometric Pressure _____

Wind _____Kts Gusts _____Kts

Weather AM   Sunny / Pt Cloudy / Cloudy / Lt Rain / Rain / Heavy Rain

Weather PM   Sunny / Pt Cloudy / Cloudy / Lt Rain / Rain / Heavy Rain

Ocean Fishing

Wind Waves Ft/s _____ / _____ Direction _____

Swells Ft/s _____ / _____ Direction _____

Time Crossed Bar _____ Water Temp _____

Notes _____

_____

River/Bay Fishing

River Flow _____CFS Water Temp _____

Water Clarity _____ Drift or Motor Boat (circle)

Notes _____

_____

Crab Pots

Location/waypoints _____

Time In _____ Time Out _____

Pots _____ # Females _____

Males _____ # Keepers _____

Notes _____

_____

Time	Location	Depth	Species "K"eeper - "R"eleased	Length	Weight	Troll, Drift, Stationary	Bait/Lure

Date _____ Time Launch _____AM/PM Time Out _____AM/PM

Port/Dock _____

Fishing Buddies _____

High Tide_____ Low Tide _____

Sunrise _____AM Sunset _____PM

Air Temp Range _____ Barometric Pressure _____

Wind _____Kts Gusts _____Kts

Weather AM   Sunny / Pt Cloudy / Cloudy / Lt Rain / Rain / Heavy Rain

Weather PM   Sunny / Pt Cloudy / Cloudy / Lt Rain / Rain / Heavy Rain

Ocean Fishing

Wind Waves Ft/s _____ /_____ Direction _____

Swells Ft/s _____ / _____ Direction _____

Time Crossed Bar _____ Water Temp _____

Notes _____

_____

River/Bay Fishing

River Flow _____CFS Water Temp _____

Water Clarity _____ Drift or Motor Boat (circle)

Notes _____

_____

Crab Pots

Location/waypoints _____

Time In _____ Time Out _____

Pots _____ # Females _____

Males _____ # Keepers _____

Notes _____

_____

Time	Location	Depth	Species "K"eeper - "R"eleased	Length	Weight	Troll, Drift, Stationary	Bait/Lure

Date _____ Time Launch _____AM/PM Time Out _____AM/PM

Port/Dock _____

Fishing Buddies _____

High Tide_____ Low Tide _____

Sunrise _____AM Sunset _____PM

Air Temp Range _____ Barometric Pressure _____

Wind _____Kts Gusts _____Kts

Weather AM   Sunny / Pt Cloudy / Cloudy / Lt Rain / Rain / Heavy Rain

Weather PM   Sunny / Pt Cloudy / Cloudy / Lt Rain / Rain / Heavy Rain

Ocean Fishing

Wind Waves Ft/s _____ /_____ Direction _____

Swells Ft/s _____ / _____ Direction _____

Time Crossed Bar _____ Water Temp _____

Notes _____

_____

River/Bay Fishing

River Flow _____CFS Water Temp _____

Water Clarity _____ Drift or Motor Boat (circle)

Notes _____

_____

Crab Pots

Location/waypoints _____

Time In _____ Time Out _____

Pots _____ # Females _____

Males _____ # Keepers _____

Notes _____

_____

Time	Location	Depth	Species "K"eeper - "R"eleased	Length	Weight	Troll, Drift, Stationary	Bait/Lure

Date _____ Time Launch _____AM/PM Time Out _____AM/PM

Port/Dock _____

Fishing Buddies _____

High Tide_____ Low Tide _____

Sunrise _____AM Sunset _____PM

Air Temp Range _____ Barometric Pressure _____

Wind _____Kts Gusts _____Kts

Weather AM   Sunny / Pt Cloudy / Cloudy / Lt Rain / Rain / Heavy Rain

Weather PM   Sunny / Pt Cloudy / Cloudy / Lt Rain / Rain / Heavy Rain

Ocean Fishing

Wind Waves Ft/s _____ /_____ Direction _____

Swells Ft/s _____ / _____ Direction _____

Time Crossed Bar _____ Water Temp _____

Notes _____

_____

River/Bay Fishing

River Flow _____CFS Water Temp _____

Water Clarity _____ Drift or Motor Boat (circle)

Notes _____

_____

Crab Pots

Location/waypoints _____

Time In _____ Time Out _____

Pots _____ # Females _____

Males _____ # Keepers _____

Notes _____

_____

Time	Location	Depth	Species "K"eeper - "R"eleased	Length	Weight	Troll, Drift, Stationary	Bait/Lure

Date _____ Time Launch _____AM/PM Time Out _____AM/PM

Port/Dock _____

Fishing Buddies _____

High Tide_____ Low Tide _____

Sunrise _____AM Sunset _____PM

Air Temp Range _____ Barometric Pressure _____

Wind _____Kts Gusts _____Kts

Weather AM   Sunny / Pt Cloudy / Cloudy / Lt Rain / Rain / Heavy Rain

Weather PM   Sunny / Pt Cloudy / Cloudy / Lt Rain / Rain / Heavy Rain

Ocean Fishing

Wind Waves Ft/s _____ / _____ Direction _____

Swells Ft/s _____ / _____ Direction _____

Time Crossed Bar _____ Water Temp _____

Notes _____

_____

River/Bay Fishing

River Flow _____CFS Water Temp _____

Water Clarity _____ Drift or Motor Boat (circle)

Notes _____

_____

Crab Pots

Location/waypoints _____

Time In _____ Time Out _____

Pots _____ # Females _____

Males _____ # Keepers _____

Notes _____

_____

Time	Location	Depth	Species "K"eeper - "R"eleased	Length	Weight	Troll, Drift, Stationary	Bait/Lure

Date _____ Time Launch _____AM/PM Time Out _____AM/PM

Port/Dock _____

Fishing Buddies _____

High Tide_____ Low Tide _____

Sunrise _____AM Sunset _____PM

Air Temp Range _____ Barometric Pressure _____

Wind _____Kts Gusts _____Kts

Weather AM   Sunny / Pt Cloudy / Cloudy / Lt Rain / Rain / Heavy Rain

Weather PM   Sunny / Pt Cloudy / Cloudy / Lt Rain / Rain / Heavy Rain

Ocean Fishing

Wind Waves Ft/s _____ / _____ Direction _____

Swells Ft/s _____ / _____ Direction _____

Time Crossed Bar _____ Water Temp _____

Notes _____

_____

River/Bay Fishing

River Flow _____CFS Water Temp _____

Water Clarity _____ Drift or Motor Boat (circle)

Notes _____

_____

Crab Pots

Location/waypoints _____

Time In _____ Time Out _____

Pots _____ # Females _____

Males _____ # Keepers _____

Notes _____

_____

Time	Location	Depth	Species "K"eeper - "R"eleased	Length	Weight	Troll, Drift, Stationary	Bait/Lure

Date _____ Time Launch _____AM/PM Time Out _____AM/PM

Port/Dock _____

Fishing Buddies _____

High Tide_____ Low Tide _____

Sunrise _____AM Sunset _____PM

Air Temp Range _____ Barometric Pressure _____

Wind _____Kts Gusts _____Kts

Weather AM   Sunny / Pt Cloudy / Cloudy / Lt Rain / Rain / Heavy Rain

Weather PM   Sunny / Pt Cloudy / Cloudy / Lt Rain / Rain / Heavy Rain

Ocean Fishing

Wind Waves Ft/s _____ / _____ Direction _____

Swells Ft/s _____ / _____ Direction _____

Time Crossed Bar _____ Water Temp _____

Notes _____

_____

River/Bay Fishing

River Flow _____CFS Water Temp _____

Water Clarity _____ Drift or Motor Boat (circle)

Notes _____

_____

Crab Pots

Location/waypoints _____

Time In _____ Time Out _____

Pots _____ # Females _____

Males _____ # Keepers _____

Notes _____

_____

Time	Location	Depth	Species "K"eeper - "R"eleased	Length	Weight	Troll, Drift, Stationary	Bait/Lure

Date _____ Time Launch _____AM/PM Time Out _____AM/PM

Port/Dock _____

Fishing Buddies _____

High Tide_____ Low Tide _____

Sunrise _____AM Sunset _____PM

Air Temp Range _____ Barometric Pressure _____

Wind _____Kts Gusts _____Kts

Weather AM   Sunny / Pt Cloudy / Cloudy / Lt Rain / Rain / Heavy Rain

Weather PM   Sunny / Pt Cloudy / Cloudy / Lt Rain / Rain / Heavy Rain

Ocean Fishing

Wind Waves Ft/s _____ / _____ Direction _____

Swells Ft/s _____ / _____ Direction _____

Time Crossed Bar _____ Water Temp _____

Notes _____

_____

River/Bay Fishing

River Flow _____CFS Water Temp _____

Water Clarity _____ Drift or Motor Boat (circle)

Notes _____

_____

Crab Pots

Location/waypoints _____

Time In _____ Time Out _____

Pots _____ # Females _____

Males _____ # Keepers _____

Notes _____

_____

Time	Location	Depth	Species "K"eeper - "R"eleased	Length	Weight	Troll, Drift, Stationary	Bait/Lure

Date _____ Time Launch _____AM/PM Time Out _____AM/PM

Port/Dock _____

Fishing Buddies _____

High Tide_____ Low Tide _____

Sunrise _____AM Sunset _____PM

Air Temp Range _____ Barometric Pressure _____

Wind _____Kts Gusts _____Kts

Weather AM   Sunny / Pt Cloudy / Cloudy / Lt Rain / Rain / Heavy Rain

Weather PM   Sunny / Pt Cloudy / Cloudy / Lt Rain / Rain / Heavy Rain

Ocean Fishing

Wind Waves Ft/s _____ /_____ Direction _____

Swells Ft/s _____ / _____ Direction _____

Time Crossed Bar _____ Water Temp _____

Notes _____

_____

River/Bay Fishing

River Flow _____CFS Water Temp _____

Water Clarity _____ Drift or Motor Boat (circle)

Notes _____

_____

Crab Pots

Location/waypoints _____

Time In _____ Time Out _____

Pots _____ # Females _____

Males _____ # Keepers _____

Notes _____

_____

Time	Location	Depth	Species "K"eeper - "R"eleased	Length	Weight	Troll, Drift, Stationary	Bait/Lure

Date _____ Time Launch _____AM/PM Time Out _____AM/PM

Port/Dock _____

Fishing Buddies _____

High Tide_____ Low Tide _____

Sunrise _____AM Sunset _____PM

Air Temp Range _____ Barometric Pressure _____

Wind _____Kts Gusts _____Kts

Weather AM   Sunny / Pt Cloudy / Cloudy / Lt Rain / Rain / Heavy Rain

Weather PM   Sunny / Pt Cloudy / Cloudy / Lt Rain / Rain / Heavy Rain

Ocean Fishing

Wind Waves Ft/s _____ /_____ Direction _____

Swells Ft/s _____ / _____ Direction _____

Time Crossed Bar _____ Water Temp _____

Notes _____

_____

River/Bay Fishing

River Flow _____CFS Water Temp _____

Water Clarity _____ Drift or Motor Boat (circle)

Notes _____

_____

Crab Pots

Location/waypoints _____

Time In _____ Time Out _____

Pots _____ # Females _____

Males _____ # Keepers _____

Notes _____

_____

Time	Location	Depth	Species "K"eeper - "R"eleased	Length	Weight	Troll, Drift, Stationary	Bait/Lure

Date _____ Time Launch _____ AM/PM Time Out _____ AM/PM

Port/Dock _____

Fishing Buddies _____

High Tide_____ Low Tide _____

Sunrise _____AM Sunset _____PM

Air Temp Range _____ Barometric Pressure _____

Wind _____Kts Gusts _____Kts

Weather AM   Sunny / Pt Cloudy / Cloudy / Lt Rain / Rain / Heavy Rain

Weather PM   Sunny / Pt Cloudy / Cloudy / Lt Rain / Rain / Heavy Rain

Ocean Fishing

Wind Waves Ft/s _____ / _____ Direction _____

Swells Ft/s _____ / _____ Direction _____

Time Crossed Bar _____ Water Temp _____

Notes _____

_____

River/Bay Fishing

River Flow _____CFS Water Temp _____

Water Clarity _____ Drift or Motor Boat (circle)

Notes _____

_____

Crab Pots

Location/waypoints _____

Time In _____ Time Out _____

Pots _____ # Females _____

Males _____ # Keepers _____

Notes _____

_____

Time	Location	Depth	Species "K"eeper - "R"eleased	Length	Weight	Troll, Drift, Stationary	Bait/Lure

Date _____ Time Launch _____AM/PM Time Out _____AM/PM

Port/Dock _____

Fishing Buddies _____

High Tide_____ Low Tide _____

Sunrise _____AM Sunset _____PM

Air Temp Range _____ Barometric Pressure _____

Wind _____Kts Gusts _____Kt

Weather AM   Sunny / Pt Cloudy / Cloudy / Lt Rain / Rain / Heavy Rain

Weather PM   Sunny / Pt Cloudy / Cloudy / Lt Rain / Rain / Heavy Rain

Ocean Fishing

Wind Waves Ft/s _____ / _____ Direction _____

Swells Ft/s _____ / _____ Direction _____

Time Crossed Bar _____ Water Temp _____

Notes _____

_____

River/Bay Fishing

River Flow _____CFS Water Temp _____

Water Clarity _____ Drift or Motor Boat (circle)

Notes _____

_____

Crab Pots

Location/waypoints _____

Time In _____ Time Out _____

Pots _____ # Females _____

Males _____ # Keepers _____

Notes _____

_____

Time	Location	Depth	Species "K"eeper - "R"eleased	Length	Weight	Troll, Drift, Stationary	Bait/Lure

Date _____ Time Launch _____AM/PM Time Out _____AM/PM

Port/Dock _____

Fishing Buddies _____

High Tide_____ Low Tide _____

Sunrise _____AM Sunset _____PM

Air Temp Range _____ Barometric Pressure _____

Wind _____Kts Gusts _____Kts

Weather AM   Sunny / Pt Cloudy / Cloudy / Lt Rain / Rain / Heavy Rain

Weather PM   Sunny / Pt Cloudy / Cloudy / Lt Rain / Rain / Heavy Rain

Ocean Fishing

Wind Waves Ft/s _____ /_____ Direction _____

Swells Ft/s _____ / _____ Direction _____

Time Crossed Bar _____ Water Temp _____

Notes _____

_____

River/Bay Fishing

River Flow _____CFS Water Temp _____

Water Clarity _____ Drift or Motor Boat (circle)

Notes _____

_____

Crab Pots

Location/waypoints _____

Time In _____ Time Out _____

Pots _____ # Females _____

Males _____ # Keepers _____

Notes _____

_____

Time	Location	Depth	Species "K"eeper - "R"eleased	Length	Weight	Troll, Drift, Stationary	Bait/Lure

Date _____ Time Launch _____AM/PM Time Out _____AM/PM

Port/Dock _____

Fishing Buddies _____

High Tide_____ Low Tide _____

Sunrise _____AM Sunset _____PM

Air Temp Range _____ Barometric Pressure _____

Wind _____Kts Gusts _____Kts

Weather AM   Sunny / Pt Cloudy / Cloudy / Lt Rain / Rain / Heavy Rain

Weather PM   Sunny / Pt Cloudy / Cloudy / Lt Rain / Rain / Heavy Rain

Ocean Fishing

Wind Waves Ft/s _____ / _____ Direction _____

Swells Ft/s _____ / _____ Direction _____

Time Crossed Bar _____ Water Temp _____

Notes _____

_____

River/Bay Fishing

River Flow _____CFS Water Temp _____

Water Clarity _____ Drift or Motor Boat (circle)

Notes _____

_____

Crab Pots

Location/waypoints _____

Time In _____ Time Out _____

Pots _____ # Females _____

Males _____ # Keepers _____

Notes _____

_____

Time	Location	Depth	Species "K"eeper - "R"eleased	Length	Weight	Troll, Drift, Stationary	Bait/Lure

Date _____ Time Launch _____AM/PM Time Out _____AM/PM

Port/Dock _____

Fishing Buddies _____

High Tide_____ Low Tide _____

Sunrise _____AM Sunset _____PM

Air Temp Range _____ Barometric Pressure _____

Wind _____Kts Gusts _____Kts

Weather AM   Sunny / Pt Cloudy / Cloudy / Lt Rain / Rain / Heavy Rain

Weather PM   Sunny / Pt Cloudy / Cloudy / Lt Rain / Rain / Heavy Rain

Ocean Fishing

Wind Waves Ft/s _____ /_____ Direction _____

Swells Ft/s _____ / _____ Direction _____

Time Crossed Bar _____ Water Temp _____

Notes _____

_____

River/Bay Fishing

River Flow _____CFS Water Temp _____

Water Clarity _____ Drift or Motor Boat (circle)

Notes _____

_____

Crab Pots

Location/waypoints _____

Time In _____ Time Out _____

Pots _____ # Females _____

Males _____ # Keepers _____

Notes _____

_____

Time	Location	Depth	Species "K"eeper - "R"eleased	Length	Weight	Troll, Drift, Stationary	Bait/Lure

Date _____ Time Launch _____AM/PM Time Out _____AM/PM

Port/Dock _____

Fishing Buddies _____

High Tide_____ Low Tide _____

Sunrise _____AM Sunset _____PM

Air Temp Range _____ Barometric Pressure _____

Wind _____Kts Gusts _____Kts

Weather AM   Sunny / Pt Cloudy / Cloudy / Lt Rain / Rain / Heavy Rain

Weather PM   Sunny / Pt Cloudy / Cloudy / Lt Rain / Rain / Heavy Rain

Ocean Fishing

Wind Waves Ft/s _____ /_____ Direction _____

Swells Ft/s _____ / _____ Direction _____

Time Crossed Bar _____ Water Temp _____

Notes _____

_____

River/Bay Fishing

River Flow _____CFS Water Temp _____

Water Clarity _____ Drift or Motor Boat (circle)

Notes _____

_____

Crab Pots

Location/waypoints _____

Time In _____ Time Out _____

Pots _____ # Females _____

Males _____ # Keepers _____

Notes _____

_____

Time	Location	Depth	Species "K"eeper - "R"eleased	Length	Weight	Troll, Drift, Stationary	Bait/Lure

Date _____ Time Launch _____AM/PM Time Out _____AM/PM

Port/Dock _____

Fishing Buddies _____

High Tide_____ Low Tide _____

Sunrise _____AM Sunset _____PM

Air Temp Range _____ Barometric Pressure _____

Wind _____Kts Gusts _____Kts

Weather AM   Sunny / Pt Cloudy / Cloudy / Lt Rain / Rain / Heavy Rain

Weather PM   Sunny / Pt Cloudy / Cloudy / Lt Rain / Rain / Heavy Rain

Ocean Fishing

Wind Waves Ft/s _____ /_____ Direction _____

Swells Ft/s _____ / _____ Direction _____

Time Crossed Bar _____ Water Temp _____

Notes _____

_____

River/Bay Fishing

River Flow _____CFS Water Temp _____

Water Clarity _____ Drift or Motor Boat (circle)

Notes _____

_____

Crab Pots

Location/waypoints _____

Time In _____ Time Out _____

Pots _____ # Females _____

Males _____ # Keepers _____

Notes _____

_____

Time	Location	Depth	Species "K"eeper - "R"eleased	Length	Weight	Troll, Drift, Stationary	Bait/Lure

Date _____ Time Launch _____AM/PM Time Out _____AM/PM

Port/Dock _____

Fishing Buddies _____

High Tide_____ Low Tide _____

Sunrise _____AM Sunset _____PM

Air Temp Range _____ Barometric Pressure _____

Wind _____Kts Gusts _____Kts

Weather AM   Sunny / Pt Cloudy / Cloudy / Lt Rain / Rain / Heavy Rain

Weather PM   Sunny / Pt Cloudy / Cloudy / Lt Rain / Rain / Heavy Rain

Ocean Fishing

Wind Waves Ft/s _____ / _____   Direction _____

Swells Ft/s _____ / _____   Direction _____

Time Crossed Bar _____   Water Temp _____

Notes _____

_____

River/Bay Fishing

River Flow _____CFS   Water Temp _____

Water Clarity _____   Drift or Motor Boat (circle)

Notes _____

_____

Crab Pots

Location/waypoints _____

Time In _____   Time Out _____

Pots _____   # Females _____

Males _____   # Keepers _____

Notes _____

_____

Time	Location	Depth	Species "K"eeper - "R"eleased	Length	Weight	Troll, Drift, Stationary	Bait/Lure

Date _____ Time Launch _____AM/PM Time Out _____AM/PM

Port/Dock _____

Fishing Buddies _____

High Tide_____ Low Tide _____

Sunrise _____AM Sunset _____PM

Air Temp Range _____ Barometric Pressure _____

Wind _____Kts Gusts _____Kts

Weather AM   Sunny / Pt Cloudy / Cloudy / Lt Rain / Rain / Heavy Rain

Weather PM   Sunny / Pt Cloudy / Cloudy / Lt Rain / Rain / Heavy Rain

Ocean Fishing

Wind Waves Ft/s _____ /_____ Direction _____

Swells Ft/s _____ / _____ Direction _____

Time Crossed Bar _____ Water Temp _____

Notes _____

_____

River/Bay Fishing

River Flow _____CFS Water Temp _____

Water Clarity _____ Drift or Motor Boat (circle)

Notes _____

_____

Crab Pots

Location/waypoints _____

Time In _____ Time Out _____

Pots _____ # Females _____

Males _____ # Keepers _____

Notes _____

_____

Time	Location	Depth	Species "K"eeper - "R"eleased	Length	Weight	Troll, Drift, Stationary	Bait/Lure

Date _____ Time Launch _____AM/PM Time Out _____AM/PM

Port/Dock _____

Fishing Buddies _____

High Tide_____ Low Tide _____

Sunrise _____AM Sunset _____PM

Air Temp Range _____ Barometric Pressure _____

Wind _____Kts Gusts _____Kt

Weather AM   Sunny / Pt Cloudy / Cloudy / Lt Rain / Rain / Heavy Rain

Weather PM   Sunny / Pt Cloudy / Cloudy / Lt Rain / Rain / Heavy Rain

Ocean Fishing

Wind Waves Ft/s _____ /_____ Direction _____

Swells Ft/s _____ / _____ Direction _____

Time Crossed Bar _____ Water Temp _____

Notes _____

_____

River/Bay Fishing

River Flow _____CFS Water Temp _____

Water Clarity _____ Drift or Motor Boat (circle)

Notes _____

_____

Crab Pots

Location/waypoints _____

Time In _____ Time Out _____

Pots _____ # Females _____

Males _____ # Keepers _____

Notes _____

_____

Time	Location	Depth	Species "K"eeper - "R"eleased	Length	Weight	Troll, Drift, Stationary	Bait/Lure

Date _____ Time Launch _____AM/PM Time Out _____AM/PM

Port/Dock _____

Fishing Buddies _____

High Tide_____ Low Tide _____

Sunrise _____AM Sunset _____PM

Air Temp Range _____ Barometric Pressure _____

Wind _____Kts Gusts _____Kts

Weather AM   Sunny / Pt Cloudy / Cloudy / Lt Rain / Rain / Heavy Rain

Weather PM   Sunny / Pt Cloudy / Cloudy / Lt Rain / Rain / Heavy Rain

Ocean Fishing

Wind Waves Ft/s _____ / _____ Direction _____

Swells Ft/s _____ / _____ Direction _____

Time Crossed Bar _____ Water Temp _____

Notes _____

_____

River/Bay Fishing

River Flow _____CFS Water Temp _____

Water Clarity _____ Drift or Motor Boat (circle)

Notes _____

_____

Crab Pots

Location/waypoints _____

Time In _____ Time Out _____

Pots _____ # Females _____

Males _____ # Keepers _____

Notes _____

_____

Time	Location	Depth	Species "K"eeper - "R"eleased	Length	Weight	Troll, Drift, Stationary	Bait/Lure

Date _____ Time Launch _____ AM/PM Time Out _____ AM/PM

Port/Dock _____

Fishing Buddies _____

High Tide_____   Low Tide _____

Sunrise _____AM   Sunset _____PM

Air Temp Range _____   Barometric Pressure _____

Wind _____Kts   Gusts _____Kt

Weather AM   Sunny / Pt Cloudy / Cloudy / Lt Rain / Rain / Heavy Rain

Weather PM   Sunny / Pt Cloudy / Cloudy / Lt Rain / Rain / Heavy Rain

Ocean Fishing

Wind Waves Ft/s _____ / _____   Direction _____

Swells Ft/s _____ / _____   Direction _____

Time Crossed Bar _____   Water Temp _____

Notes _____

_____

River/Bay Fishing

River Flow _____CFS   Water Temp _____

Water Clarity _____   Drift or Motor Boat (circle)

Notes _____

_____

Crab Pots

Location/waypoints _____

Time In _____   Time Out _____

Pots _____   # Females _____

Males _____   # Keepers _____

Notes _____

_____

Time	Location	Depth	Species "K"eeper - "R"eleased	Length	Weight	Troll, Drift, Stationary	Bait/Lure

Date _____ Time Launch _____AM/PM Time Out _____AM/PM

Port/Dock _____

Fishing Buddies _____

High Tide_____ Low Tide _____

Sunrise _____AM Sunset _____PM

Air Temp Range _____ Barometric Pressure _____

Wind _____Kts Gusts _____Kts

Weather AM   Sunny / Pt Cloudy / Cloudy / Lt Rain / Rain / Heavy Rain

Weather PM   Sunny / Pt Cloudy / Cloudy / Lt Rain / Rain / Heavy Rain

Ocean Fishing

Wind Waves Ft/s _____ / _____ Direction _____

Swells Ft/s _____ / _____ Direction _____

Time Crossed Bar _____ Water Temp _____

Notes _____

_____

River/Bay Fishing

River Flow _____CFS Water Temp _____

Water Clarity _____ Drift or Motor Boat (circle)

Notes _____

_____

Crab Pots

Location/waypoints _____

Time In _____ Time Out _____

Pots _____ # Females _____

Males _____ # Keepers _____

Notes _____

_____

Time	Location	Depth	Species "K"eeper - "R"eleased	Length	Weight	Troll, Drift, Stationary	Bait/Lure

Date _____ Time Launch _____AM/PM Time Out _____AM/PM

Port/Dock _____

Fishing Buddies _____

High Tide_____   Low Tide _____

Sunrise _____AM   Sunset _____PM

Air Temp Range _____   Barometric Pressure _____

Wind _____Kts   Gusts _____Kts

Weather AM   Sunny / Pt Cloudy / Cloudy / Lt Rain / Rain / Heavy Rain

Weather PM   Sunny / Pt Cloudy / Cloudy / Lt Rain / Rain / Heavy Rain

Ocean Fishing

Wind Waves Ft/s _____ /_____   Direction _____

Swells Ft/s _____ / _____   Direction _____

Time Crossed Bar _____   Water Temp _____

Notes _____

_____

River/Bay Fishing

River Flow _____CFS   Water Temp _____

Water Clarity _____   Drift or Motor Boat (circle)

Notes _____

_____

Crab Pots

Location/waypoints _____

Time In _____   Time Out _____

Pots _____   # Females _____

Males _____   # Keepers _____

Notes _____

_____

Time	Location	Depth	Species "K"eeper - "R"eleased	Length	Weight	Troll, Drift, Stationary	Bait/Lure

Date _____ Time Launch _____AM/PM Time Out _____AM/PM

Port/Dock _____

Fishing Buddies _____

High Tide_____ Low Tide _____

Sunrise _____AM Sunset _____PM

Air Temp Range _____ Barometric Pressure _____

Wind _____Kts Gusts _____Kt

Weather AM   Sunny / Pt Cloudy / Cloudy / Lt Rain / Rain / Heavy Rain

Weather PM   Sunny / Pt Cloudy / Cloudy / Lt Rain / Rain / Heavy Rain

Ocean Fishing

Wind Waves Ft/s _____ / _____ Direction _____

Swells Ft/s _____ / _____ Direction _____

Time Crossed Bar _____ Water Temp _____

Notes _____

_____

River/Bay Fishing

River Flow _____CFS Water Temp _____

Water Clarity _____ Drift or Motor Boat (circle)

Notes _____

_____

Crab Pots

Location/waypoints _____

Time In _____ Time Out _____

Pots _____ # Females _____

Males _____ # Keepers _____

Notes _____

_____

Time	Location	Depth	Species "K"eeper - "R"eleased	Length	Weight	Troll, Drift, Stationary	Bait/Lure

Date _____ Time Launch _____AM/PM Time Out _____AM/PM

Port/Dock _____

Fishing Buddies _____

High Tide_____ Low Tide _____

Sunrise _____AM Sunset _____PM

Air Temp Range _____ Barometric Pressure _____

Wind _____Kts Gusts _____Kts

Weather AM   Sunny / Pt Cloudy / Cloudy / Lt Rain / Rain / Heavy Rain

Weather PM   Sunny / Pt Cloudy / Cloudy / Lt Rain / Rain / Heavy Rain

Ocean Fishing

Wind Waves Ft/s _____ /_____ Direction _____

Swells Ft/s _____ / _____ Direction _____

Time Crossed Bar _____ Water Temp _____

Notes _____

_____

River/Bay Fishing

River Flow _____CFS Water Temp _____

Water Clarity _____ Drift or Motor Boat (circle)

Notes _____

_____

Crab Pots

Location/waypoints _____

Time In _____ Time Out _____

Pots _____ # Females _____

Males _____ # Keepers _____

Notes _____

_____

Time	Location	Depth	Species "K"eeper - "R"eleased	Length	Weight	Troll, Drift, Stationary	Bait/Lure

Date _____ Time Launch _____AM/PM Time Out _____AM/PM

Port/Dock _____

Fishing Buddies _____

High Tide_____   Low Tide _____

Sunrise _____AM   Sunset _____PM

Air Temp Range _____   Barometric Pressure _____

Wind _____Kts   Gusts _____Kts

Weather AM   Sunny / Pt Cloudy / Cloudy / Lt Rain / Rain / Heavy Rain

Weather PM   Sunny / Pt Cloudy / Cloudy / Lt Rain / Rain / Heavy Rain

Ocean Fishing

Wind Waves Ft/s _____ / _____   Direction _____

Swells Ft/s _____ / _____   Direction _____

Time Crossed Bar _____   Water Temp _____

Notes _____

_____

River/Bay Fishing

River Flow _____CFS   Water Temp _____

Water Clarity _____   Drift or Motor Boat (circle)

Notes _____

_____

Crab Pots

Location/waypoints _____

Time In _____   Time Out _____

Pots _____   # Females _____

Males _____   # Keepers _____

Notes _____

_____

Time	Location	Depth	Species "K"eeper - "R"eleased	Length	Weight	Troll, Drift, Stationary	Bait/Lure

Date _____ Time Launch _____AM/PM Time Out _____AM/PM

Port/Dock _____

Fishing Buddies _____

High Tide_____ Low Tide _____

Sunrise _____AM Sunset _____PM

Air Temp Range _____ Barometric Pressure _____

Wind _____Kts Gusts _____Kts

Weather AM   Sunny / Pt Cloudy / Cloudy / Lt Rain / Rain / Heavy Rain

Weather PM   Sunny / Pt Cloudy / Cloudy / Lt Rain / Rain / Heavy Rain

Ocean Fishing

Wind Waves Ft/s _____ / _____ Direction _____

Swells Ft/s _____ / _____ Direction _____

Time Crossed Bar _____ Water Temp _____

Notes _____

_____

River/Bay Fishing

River Flow _____CFS Water Temp _____

Water Clarity _____ Drift or Motor Boat (circle)

Notes _____

_____

Crab Pots

Location/waypoints _____

Time In _____ Time Out _____

Pots _____ # Females _____

Males _____ # Keepers _____

Notes _____

_____

Time	Location	Depth	Species "K"eeper - "R"eleased	Length	Weight	Troll, Drift, Stationary	Bait/Lure

Date _____ Time Launch _____ AM/PM Time Out _____ AM/PM

Port/Dock _____

Fishing Buddies _____

High Tide_____   Low Tide _____

Sunrise _____AM   Sunset _____PM

Air Temp Range _____   Barometric Pressure _____

Wind _____Kts   Gusts _____Kts

Weather AM   Sunny / Pt Cloudy / Cloudy / Lt Rain / Rain / Heavy Rain

Weather PM   Sunny / Pt Cloudy / Cloudy / Lt Rain / Rain / Heavy Rain

Ocean Fishing

Wind Waves Ft/s _____ / _____   Direction _____

Swells Ft/s _____ / _____   Direction _____

Time Crossed Bar _____   Water Temp _____

Notes _____

_____

River/Bay Fishing

River Flow _____CFS   Water Temp _____

Water Clarity _____   Drift or Motor Boat (circle)

Notes _____

_____

Crab Pots

Location/waypoints _____

Time In _____   Time Out _____

Pots _____   # Females _____

Males _____   # Keepers _____

Notes _____

_____

Time	Location	Depth	Species "K"eeper - "R"eleased	Length	Weight	Troll, Drift, Stationary	Bait/Lure

Date _____ Time Launch _____AM/PM Time Out _____AM/PM

Port/Dock _____

Fishing Buddies _____

High Tide_____ Low Tide _____

Sunrise _____AM Sunset _____PM

Air Temp Range _____ Barometric Pressure _____

Wind _____Kts Gusts _____Kts

    Weather AM   Sunny / Pt Cloudy / Cloudy / Lt Rain / Rain / Heavy Rain

    Weather PM   Sunny / Pt Cloudy / Cloudy / Lt Rain / Rain / Heavy Rain

Ocean Fishing

Wind Waves Ft/s _____ / _____ Direction _____

Swells Ft/s _____ / _____ Direction _____

Time Crossed Bar _____ Water Temp _____

Notes _____

_____

River/Bay Fishing

River Flow _____CFS Water Temp _____

Water Clarity _____ Drift or Motor Boat (circle)

Notes _____

_____

Crab Pots

Location/waypoints _____

Time In _____ Time Out _____

Pots _____ # Females _____

Males _____ # Keepers _____

Notes _____

_____

Time	Location	Depth	Species "K"eeper – "R"eleased	Length	Weight	Troll, Drift, Stationary	Bait/Lure

Date _____ Time Launch _____ AM/PM Time Out _____ AM/PM

Port/Dock _____

Fishing Buddies _____

High Tide_____   Low Tide _____

Sunrise _____AM   Sunset _____PM

Air Temp Range _____   Barometric Pressure _____

Wind _____Kts   Gusts _____Kt

Weather AM   Sunny / Pt Cloudy / Cloudy / Lt Rain / Rain / Heavy Rain

Weather PM   Sunny / Pt Cloudy / Cloudy / Lt Rain / Rain / Heavy Rain

Ocean Fishing

Wind Waves Ft/s _____ / _____   Direction _____

Swells Ft/s _____ / _____   Direction _____

Time Crossed Bar _____   Water Temp _____

Notes _____

_____

River/Bay Fishing

River Flow _____CFS   Water Temp _____

Water Clarity _____   Drift or Motor Boat (circle)

Notes _____

_____

Crab Pots

Location/waypoints _____

Time In _____   Time Out _____

Pots _____   # Females _____

Males _____   # Keepers _____

Notes _____

_____

Time	Location	Depth	Species "K"eeper - "R"eleased	Length	Weight	Troll, Drift, Stationary	Bait/Lure

Date _____ Time Launch _____AM/PM Time Out _____AM/PM

Port/Dock _____

Fishing Buddies _____

High Tide_____ Low Tide _____

Sunrise _____AM Sunset _____PM

Air Temp Range _____ Barometric Pressure _____

Wind _____Kts Gusts _____Kt.

Weather AM   Sunny / Pt Cloudy / Cloudy / Lt Rain / Rain / Heavy Rain

Weather PM   Sunny / Pt Cloudy / Cloudy / Lt Rain / Rain / Heavy Rain

Ocean Fishing

Wind Waves Ft/s _____ /_____ Direction _____

Swells Ft/s _____ / _____ Direction _____

Time Crossed Bar _____ Water Temp _____

Notes _____

_____

River/Bay Fishing

River Flow _____CFS Water Temp _____

Water Clarity _____ Drift or Motor Boat (circle)

Notes _____

_____

Crab Pots

Location/waypoints _____

Time In _____ Time Out _____

Pots _____ # Females _____

Males _____ # Keepers _____

Notes _____

_____

Time	Location	Depth	Species "K"eeper - "R"eleased	Length	Weight	Troll, Drift, Stationary	Bait/Lure

Date _____ Time Launch _____AM/PM Time Out _____AM/PM

Port/Dock _____

Fishing Buddies _____

High Tide_____ Low Tide _____

Sunrise _____AM Sunset _____PM

Air Temp Range _____ Barometric Pressure _____

Wind _____Kts Gusts _____Kt

Weather AM   Sunny / Pt Cloudy / Cloudy / Lt Rain / Rain / Heavy Rain

Weather PM   Sunny / Pt Cloudy / Cloudy / Lt Rain / Rain / Heavy Rain

Ocean Fishing

Wind Waves Ft/s _____ /_____ Direction _____

Swells Ft/s _____ / _____ Direction _____

Time Crossed Bar _____ Water Temp _____

Notes _____

_____

River/Bay Fishing

River Flow _____CFS Water Temp _____

Water Clarity _____ Drift or Motor Boat (circle)

Notes _____

_____

Crab Pots

Location/waypoints _____

Time In _____ Time Out _____

Pots _____ # Females _____

Males _____ # Keepers _____

Notes _____

_____

Time	Location	Depth	Species "K"eeper - "R"eleased	Length	Weight	Troll, Drift, Stationary	Bait/Lure

Date _____ Time Launch _____AM/PM Time Out _____AM/PM

Port/Dock _____

Fishing Buddies _____

High Tide_____ Low Tide _____

Sunrise _____AM Sunset _____PM

Air Temp Range _____ Barometric Pressure _____

Wind _____Kts Gusts _____Kts

Weather AM   Sunny / Pt Cloudy / Cloudy / Lt Rain / Rain / Heavy Rain

Weather PM   Sunny / Pt Cloudy / Cloudy / Lt Rain / Rain / Heavy Rain

Ocean Fishing

Wind Waves Ft/s _____ / _____ Direction _____

Swells Ft/s _____ / _____ Direction _____

Time Crossed Bar _____ Water Temp _____

Notes _____

_____

River/Bay Fishing

River Flow _____CFS Water Temp _____

Water Clarity _____ Drift or Motor Boat (circle)

Notes _____

_____

Crab Pots

Location/waypoints _____

Time In _____ Time Out _____

Pots _____ # Females _____

Males _____ # Keepers _____

Notes _____

_____

Time	Location	Depth	Species "K"eeper - "R"eleased	Length	Weight	Troll, Drift, Stationary	Bait/Lure

Date _____ Time Launch _____AM/PM Time Out _____AM/PM

Port/Dock _____

Fishing Buddies _____

High Tide_____ Low Tide _____

Sunrise _____AM Sunset _____PM

Air Temp Range _____ Barometric Pressure _____

Wind _____Kts Gusts _____Kt

Weather AM   Sunny / Pt Cloudy / Cloudy / Lt Rain / Rain / Heavy Rain

Weather PM   Sunny / Pt Cloudy / Cloudy / Lt Rain / Rain / Heavy Rain

Ocean Fishing

Wind Waves Ft/s _____ /_____ Direction _____

Swells Ft/s _____ / _____ Direction _____

Time Crossed Bar _____ Water Temp _____

Notes _____

_____

River/Bay Fishing

River Flow _____CFS Water Temp _____

Water Clarity _____ Drift or Motor Boat (circle)

Notes _____

_____

Crab Pots

Location/waypoints _____

Time In _____ Time Out _____

Pots _____ # Females _____

Males _____ # Keepers _____

Notes _____

_____

Time	Location	Depth	Species "K"eeper - "R"eleased	Length	Weight	Troll, Drift, Stationary	Bait/Lure

Date _____ Time Launch _____ AM/PM Time Out _____ AM/PM

Port/Dock _____

Fishing Buddies _____

High Tide_____ Low Tide _____

Sunrise _____AM Sunset _____PM

Air Temp Range _____ Barometric Pressure _____

Wind _____Kts Gusts _____Kts

Weather AM   Sunny / Pt Cloudy / Cloudy / Lt Rain / Rain / Heavy Rain

Weather PM   Sunny / Pt Cloudy / Cloudy / Lt Rain / Rain / Heavy Rain

Ocean Fishing

Wind Waves Ft/s _____ /_____ Direction _____

Swells Ft/s _____ / _____ Direction _____

Time Crossed Bar _____ Water Temp _____

Notes _____

_____

River/Bay Fishing

River Flow _____CFS Water Temp _____

Water Clarity _____ Drift or Motor Boat (circle)

Notes _____

_____

Crab Pots

Location/waypoints _____

Time In _____ Time Out _____

Pots _____ # Females _____

Males _____ # Keepers _____

Notes _____

_____

Time	Location	Depth	Species "K"eeper - "R"eleased	Length	Weight	Troll, Drift, Stationary	Bait/Lure

Date _____ Time Launch _____AM/PM Time Out _____AM/PM

Port/Dock _____

Fishing Buddies _____

High Tide_____ Low Tide _____

Sunrise _____AM Sunset _____PM

Air Temp Range _____ Barometric Pressure _____

Wind _____Kts Gusts _____Kt

Weather AM   Sunny / Pt Cloudy / Cloudy / Lt Rain / Rain / Heavy Rain

Weather PM   Sunny / Pt Cloudy / Cloudy / Lt Rain / Rain / Heavy Rain

Ocean Fishing

Wind Waves Ft/s _____ /_____   Direction _____

Swells Ft/s _____ / _____   Direction _____

Time Crossed Bar _____   Water Temp _____

Notes _____

_____

River/Bay Fishing

River Flow _____CFS   Water Temp _____

Water Clarity _____   Drift or Motor Boat (circle)

Notes _____

_____

Crab Pots

Location/waypoints _____

Time In _____ Time Out _____

Pots _____ # Females _____

Males _____ # Keepers _____

Notes _____

_____

Time	Location	Depth	Species "K"eeper - "R"eleased	Length	Weight	Troll, Drift, Stationary	Bait/Lure

Date _____ Time Launch _____AM/PM Time Out _____AM/PM

Port/Dock _____

Fishing Buddies _____

High Tide_____ Low Tide _____

Sunrise _____AM Sunset _____PM

Air Temp Range _____ Barometric Pressure _____

Wind _____Kts Gusts _____Kt

Weather AM   Sunny / Pt Cloudy / Cloudy / Lt Rain / Rain / Heavy Rain

Weather PM   Sunny / Pt Cloudy / Cloudy / Lt Rain / Rain / Heavy Rain

Ocean Fishing

Wind Waves Ft/s _____ /_____ Direction _____

Swells Ft/s _____ / _____ Direction _____

Time Crossed Bar _____ Water Temp _____

Notes _____

_____

River/Bay Fishing

River Flow _____CFS Water Temp _____

Water Clarity _____ Drift or Motor Boat (circle)

Notes _____

_____

Crab Pots

Location/waypoints _____

Time In _____ Time Out _____

Pots _____ # Females _____

Males _____ # Keepers _____

Notes _____

_____

Time	Location	Depth	Species "K"eeper – "R"eleased	Length	Weight	Troll, Drift, Stationary	Bait/Lure

Date _____ Time Launch _____AM/PM Time Out _____AM/PM

Port/Dock _____

Fishing Buddies _____

High Tide_____ Low Tide _____

Sunrise _____AM Sunset _____PM

Air Temp Range _____ Barometric Pressure _____

Wind _____Kts Gusts _____Kt

Weather AM   Sunny / Pt Cloudy / Cloudy / Lt Rain / Rain / Heavy Rain

Weather PM   Sunny / Pt Cloudy / Cloudy / Lt Rain / Rain / Heavy Rain

Ocean Fishing

Wind Waves Ft/s _____ /_____ Direction _____

Swells Ft/s _____ / _____ Direction _____

Time Crossed Bar _____ Water Temp _____

Notes _____

_____

River/Bay Fishing

River Flow _____CFS Water Temp _____

Water Clarity _____ Drift or Motor Boat (circle)

Notes _____

_____

Crab Pots

Location/waypoints _____

Time In _____ Time Out _____

Pots _____ # Females _____

Males _____ # Keepers _____

Notes _____

_____

Time	Location	Depth	Species "K"eeper - "R"eleased	Length	Weight	Troll, Drift, Stationary	Bait/Lure

Date _____ Time Launch _____AM/PM Time Out _____AM/PM

Port/Dock _____

Fishing Buddies _____

High Tide_____ Low Tide _____

Sunrise _____AM Sunset _____PM

Air Temp Range _____ Barometric Pressure _____

Wind _____Kts Gusts _____Kt

Weather AM   Sunny / Pt Cloudy / Cloudy / Lt Rain / Rain / Heavy Rain

Weather PM   Sunny / Pt Cloudy / Cloudy / Lt Rain / Rain / Heavy Rain

Ocean Fishing

Wind Waves Ft/s _____ /_____ Direction _____

Swells Ft/s _____ / _____ Direction _____

Time Crossed Bar _____ Water Temp _____

Notes _____

_____

River/Bay Fishing

River Flow _____CFS Water Temp _____

Water Clarity _____ Drift or Motor Boat (circle)

Notes _____

_____

Crab Pots

Location/waypoints _____

Time In _____ Time Out _____

Pots _____ # Females _____

Males _____ # Keepers _____

Notes _____

_____

Time	Location	Depth	Species "K"eeper - "R"eleased	Length	Weight	Troll, Drift, Stationary	Bait/Lure

Date _____ Time Launch _____ AM/PM Time Out _____ AM/PM

Port/Dock _____

Fishing Buddies _____

High Tide_____ Low Tide _____

Sunrise _____AM Sunset _____PM

Air Temp Range _____ Barometric Pressure _____

Wind _____Kts Gusts _____Kt

Weather AM   Sunny / Pt Cloudy / Cloudy / Lt Rain / Rain / Heavy Rain

Weather PM   Sunny / Pt Cloudy / Cloudy / Lt Rain / Rain / Heavy Rain

Ocean Fishing

Wind Waves Ft/s _____ / _____   Direction _____

Swells Ft/s _____ / _____   Direction _____

Time Crossed Bar _____   Water Temp _____

Notes _____

_____

River/Bay Fishing

River Flow _____CFS   Water Temp _____

Water Clarity _____   Drift or Motor Boat (circle)

Notes _____

_____

Crab Pots

Location/waypoints _____

Time In _____   Time Out _____

Pots _____   # Females _____

Males _____   # Keepers _____

Notes _____

_____

Time	Location	Depth	Species "K"eeper – "R"eleased	Length	Weight	Troll, Drift, Stationary	Bait/Lure

Date _____ Time Launch _____AM/PM Time Out _____AM/PM

Port/Dock _____

Fishing Buddies _____

High Tide_____ Low Tide _____

Sunrise _____AM Sunset _____PM

Air Temp Range _____ Barometric Pressure _____

Wind _____Kts Gusts _____Kts

Weather AM   Sunny / Pt Cloudy / Cloudy / Lt Rain / Rain / Heavy Rain

Weather PM   Sunny / Pt Cloudy / Cloudy / Lt Rain / Rain / Heavy Rain

Ocean Fishing

Wind Waves Ft/s _____ /_____ Direction _____

Swells Ft/s _____ / _____ Direction _____

Time Crossed Bar _____ Water Temp _____

Notes _____

_____

River/Bay Fishing

River Flow _____CFS Water Temp _____

Water Clarity _____ Drift or Motor Boat (circle)

Notes _____

_____

Crab Pots

Location/waypoints _____

Time In _____ Time Out _____

Pots _____ # Females _____

Males _____ # Keepers _____

Notes _____

_____

Time	Location	Depth	Species "K"eeper - "R"eleased	Length	Weight	Troll, Drift, Stationary	Bait/Lure

Date _____ Time Launch _____AM/PM Time Out _____AM/PM

Port/Dock _____

Fishing Buddies _____

High Tide_____ Low Tide _____

Sunrise _____AM Sunset _____PM

Air Temp Range _____ Barometric Pressure _____

Wind _____Kts Gusts _____Kts

Weather AM   Sunny / Pt Cloudy / Cloudy / Lt Rain / Rain / Heavy Rain

Weather PM   Sunny / Pt Cloudy / Cloudy / Lt Rain / Rain / Heavy Rain

Ocean Fishing

Wind Waves Ft/s _____ /_____ Direction _____

Swells Ft/s _____ / _____ Direction _____

Time Crossed Bar _____ Water Temp _____

Notes _____

_____

River/Bay Fishing

River Flow _____CFS Water Temp _____

Water Clarity _____ Drift or Motor Boat (circle)

Notes _____

_____

Crab Pots

Location/waypoints _____

Time In _____ Time Out _____

Pots _____ # Females _____

Males _____ # Keepers _____

Notes _____

_____

Time	Location	Depth	Species "K"eeper - "R"eleased	Length	Weight	Troll, Drift, Stationary	Bait/Lure

Date _____ Time Launch _____ AM/PM Time Out _____ AM/PM

Port/Dock _____

Fishing Buddies _____

High Tide_____ Low Tide _____

Sunrise _____AM Sunset _____PM

Air Temp Range _____ Barometric Pressure _____

Wind _____Kts Gusts _____Kts

Weather AM   Sunny / Pt Cloudy / Cloudy / Lt Rain / Rain / Heavy Rain

Weather PM   Sunny / Pt Cloudy / Cloudy / Lt Rain / Rain / Heavy Rain

Ocean Fishing

Wind Waves Ft/s _____ /_____ Direction _____

Swells Ft/s _____ / _____ Direction _____

Time Crossed Bar _____ Water Temp _____

Notes _____

_____

River/Bay Fishing

River Flow _____CFS Water Temp _____

Water Clarity _____ Drift or Motor Boat (circle)

Notes _____

_____

Crab Pots

Location/waypoints _____

Time In _____ Time Out _____

Pots _____ # Females _____

Males _____ # Keepers _____

Notes _____

_____

Time	Location	Depth	Species "K"eeper - "R"eleased	Length	Weight	Troll, Drift, Stationary	Bait/Lure

Date _____ Time Launch _____AM/PM Time Out _____AM/PM

Port/Dock _____

Fishing Buddies _____

High Tide_____ Low Tide _____

Sunrise _____AM Sunset _____PM

Air Temp Range _____ Barometric Pressure _____

Wind _____Kts Gusts _____Kts

Weather AM   Sunny / Pt Cloudy / Cloudy / Lt Rain / Rain / Heavy Rain

Weather PM   Sunny / Pt Cloudy / Cloudy / Lt Rain / Rain / Heavy Rain

Ocean Fishing

Wind Waves Ft/s _____ /_____ Direction _____

Swells Ft/s _____ / _____ Direction _____

Time Crossed Bar _____ Water Temp _____

Notes _____

_____

River/Bay Fishing

River Flow _____CFS Water Temp _____

Water Clarity _____ Drift or Motor Boat (circle)

Notes _____

_____

Crab Pots

Location/waypoints _____

Time In _____ Time Out _____

Pots _____ # Females _____

Males _____ # Keepers _____

Notes _____

_____

Time	Location	Depth	Species "K"eeper - "R"eleased	Length	Weight	Troll, Drift, Stationary	Bait/Lure

Date _____ Time Launch _____AM/PM Time Out _____AM/PM

Port/Dock _____

Fishing Buddies _____

High Tide_____ Low Tide _____

Sunrise _____AM Sunset _____PM

Air Temp Range _____ Barometric Pressure _____

Wind _____Kts Gusts _____Kts

Weather AM   Sunny / Pt Cloudy / Cloudy / Lt Rain / Rain / Heavy Rain

Weather PM   Sunny / Pt Cloudy / Cloudy / Lt Rain / Rain / Heavy Rain

Ocean Fishing

Wind Waves Ft/s _____ /_____ Direction _____

Swells Ft/s _____ / _____ Direction _____

Time Crossed Bar _____ Water Temp _____

Notes _____

_____

River/Bay Fishing

River Flow _____CFS Water Temp _____

Water Clarity _____ Drift or Motor Boat (circle)

Notes _____

_____

Crab Pots

Location/waypoints _____

Time In _____ Time Out _____

Pots _____ # Females _____

Males _____ # Keepers _____

Notes _____

_____

Time	Location	Depth	Species "K"eeper - "R"eleased	Length	Weight	Troll, Drift, Stationary	Bait/Lure

Date _____ Time Launch _____AM/PM Time Out _____AM/PM

Port/Dock _____

Fishing Buddies _____

High Tide_____ Low Tide _____

Sunrise _____AM Sunset _____PM

Air Temp Range _____ Barometric Pressure _____

Wind _____Kts Gusts _____Kts

Weather AM   Sunny / Pt Cloudy / Cloudy / Lt Rain / Rain / Heavy Rain

Weather PM   Sunny / Pt Cloudy / Cloudy / Lt Rain / Rain / Heavy Rain

Ocean Fishing

Wind Waves Ft/s _____ /_____ Direction _____

Swells Ft/s _____ / _____ Direction _____

Time Crossed Bar _____ Water Temp _____

Notes _____

_____

River/Bay Fishing

River Flow _____CFS Water Temp _____

Water Clarity _____ Drift or Motor Boat (circle)

Notes _____

_____

Crab Pots

Location/waypoints _____

Time In _____ Time Out _____

Pots _____ # Females _____

Males _____ # Keepers _____

Notes _____

_____

Time	Location	Depth	Species "K"eeper - "R"eleased	Length	Weight	Troll, Drift, Stationary	Bait/Lure

Date _____ Time Launch _____ AM/PM Time Out _____ AM/PM

Port/Dock _____

Fishing Buddies _____

High Tide_____   Low Tide _____

Sunrise _____ AM   Sunset _____ PM

Air Temp Range _____   Barometric Pressure _____

Wind _____ Kts   Gusts _____ Kt

Weather AM   Sunny / Pt Cloudy / Cloudy / Lt Rain / Rain / Heavy Rain

Weather PM   Sunny / Pt Cloudy / Cloudy / Lt Rain / Rain / Heavy Rain

Ocean Fishing

Wind Waves Ft/s _____ / _____   Direction _____

Swells Ft/s _____ / _____   Direction _____

Time Crossed Bar _____   Water Temp _____

Notes _____

_____

River/Bay Fishing

River Flow _____ CFS   Water Temp _____

Water Clarity _____   Drift or Motor Boat (circle)

Notes _____

_____

Crab Pots

Location/waypoints _____

Time In _____   Time Out _____

Pots _____   # Females _____

Males _____   # Keepers _____

Notes _____

_____

Time	Location	Depth	Species "K"eeper - "R"eleased	Length	Weight	Troll, Drift, Stationary	Bait/Lure

Date _____ Time Launch _____AM/PM Time Out _____ AM/PM

Port/Dock _____

Fishing Buddies _____

High Tide_____ Low Tide _____

Sunrise _____AM Sunset _____PM

Air Temp Range _____ Barometric Pressure _____

Wind _____Kts Gusts _____Kt

Weather AM   Sunny / Pt Cloudy / Cloudy / Lt Rain / Rain / Heavy Rain

Weather PM   Sunny / Pt Cloudy / Cloudy / Lt Rain / Rain / Heavy Rain

Ocean Fishing

Wind Waves Ft/s _____ /_____   Direction _____

Swells Ft/s _____ / _____   Direction _____

Time Crossed Bar _____   Water Temp _____

Notes _____

_____

River/Bay Fishing

River Flow _____CFS   Water Temp _____

Water Clarity _____   Drift or Motor Boat (circle)

Notes _____

_____

Crab Pots

Location/waypoints _____

Time In _____   Time Out _____

Pots _____   # Females _____

Males _____   # Keepers _____

Notes _____

_____

Time	Location	Depth	Species "K"eeper - "R"eleased	Length	Weight	Troll, Drift, Stationary	Bait/Lure

Date _____ Time Launch _____AM/PM Time Out _____AM/PM

Port/Dock _____

Fishing Buddies _____

High Tide_____ Low Tide _____

Sunrise _____AM Sunset _____PM

Air Temp Range _____ Barometric Pressure _____

Wind _____Kts Gusts _____Kts

Weather AM   Sunny / Pt Cloudy / Cloudy / Lt Rain / Rain / Heavy Rain

Weather PM   Sunny / Pt Cloudy / Cloudy / Lt Rain / Rain / Heavy Rain

Ocean Fishing

Wind Waves Ft/s _____ /_____   Direction _____

Swells Ft/s _____ / _____   Direction _____

Time Crossed Bar _____   Water Temp _____

Notes _____

_____

River/Bay Fishing

River Flow _____CFS   Water Temp _____

Water Clarity _____   Drift or Motor Boat (circle)

Notes _____

_____

Crab Pots

Location/waypoints _____

Time In _____   Time Out _____

Pots _____   # Females _____

Males _____   # Keepers _____

Notes _____

_____

Time	Location	Depth	Species "K"eeper – "R"eleased	Length	Weight	Troll, Drift, Stationary	Bait/Lure

Date _____ Time Launch _____AM/PM Time Out _____AM/PM

Port/Dock _____

Fishing Buddies _____

High Tide_____ Low Tide _____

Sunrise _____AM Sunset _____PM

Air Temp Range _____ Barometric Pressure _____

Wind _____Kts Gusts _____Kts

Weather AM   Sunny / Pt Cloudy / Cloudy / Lt Rain / Rain / Heavy Rain

Weather PM   Sunny / Pt Cloudy / Cloudy / Lt Rain / Rain / Heavy Rain

Ocean Fishing

Wind Waves Ft/s _____ /_____ Direction _____

Swells Ft/s _____ / _____ Direction _____

Time Crossed Bar _____ Water Temp _____

Notes _____

_____

River/Bay Fishing

River Flow _____CFS Water Temp _____

Water Clarity _____ Drift or Motor Boat (circle)

Notes _____

_____

Crab Pots

Location/waypoints _____

Time In _____ Time Out _____

Pots _____ # Females _____

Males _____ # Keepers _____

Notes _____

_____

Time	Location	Depth	Species "K"eeper - "R"eleased	Length	Weight	Troll, Drift, Stationary	Bait/Lure

Date _____ Time Launch _____AM/PM Time Out _____AM/PM

Port/Dock _____

Fishing Buddies _____

High Tide_____   Low Tide _____

Sunrise _____AM   Sunset _____PM

Air Temp Range _____   Barometric Pressure _____

Wind _____Kts   Gusts _____Kts

Weather AM   Sunny / Pt Cloudy / Cloudy / Lt Rain / Rain / Heavy Rain

Weather PM   Sunny / Pt Cloudy / Cloudy / Lt Rain / Rain / Heavy Rain

Ocean Fishing

Wind Waves Ft/s _____ /_____   Direction _____

Swells Ft/s _____ / _____   Direction _____

Time Crossed Bar _____   Water Temp _____

Notes _____

_____

River/Bay Fishing

River Flow _____CFS   Water Temp _____

Water Clarity _____   Drift or Motor Boat (circle)

Notes _____

_____

Crab Pots

Location/waypoints _____

Time In _____   Time Out _____

Pots _____   # Females _____

Males _____   # Keepers _____

Notes _____

_____

Time	Location	Depth	Species "K"eeper - "R"eleased	Length	Weight	Troll, Drift, Stationary	Bait/Lure

Date _____ Time Launch _____AM/PM Time Out _____AM/PM

Port/Dock _____

Fishing Buddies _____

High Tide_____ Low Tide _____

Sunrise _____AM Sunset _____PM

Air Temp Range _____ Barometric Pressure _____

Wind _____Kts Gusts _____Kts

Weather AM   Sunny / Pt Cloudy / Cloudy / Lt Rain / Rain / Heavy Rain

Weather PM   Sunny / Pt Cloudy / Cloudy / Lt Rain / Rain / Heavy Rain

Ocean Fishing

Wind Waves Ft/s _____ /_____ Direction _____

Swells Ft/s _____ / _____ Direction _____

Time Crossed Bar _____ Water Temp _____

Notes _____

_____

River/Bay Fishing

River Flow _____CFS Water Temp _____

Water Clarity _____ Drift or Motor Boat (circle)

Notes _____

_____

Crab Pots

Location/waypoints _____

Time In _____ Time Out _____

Pots _____ # Females _____

Males _____ # Keepers _____

Notes _____

_____

Time	Location	Depth	Species "K"eeper - "R"eleased	Length	Weight	Troll, Drift, Stationary	Bait/Lure

Date _____ Time Launch _____ AM/PM Time Out _____ AM/PM

Port/Dock _____

Fishing Buddies _____

High Tide_____ Low Tide _____

Sunrise _____AM Sunset _____PM

Air Temp Range _____ Barometric Pressure _____

Wind _____Kts Gusts _____Kts

Weather AM   Sunny / Pt Cloudy / Cloudy / Lt Rain / Rain / Heavy Rain

Weather PM   Sunny / Pt Cloudy / Cloudy / Lt Rain / Rain / Heavy Rain

Ocean Fishing

Wind Waves Ft/s _____ /_____ Direction _____

Swells Ft/s _____ / _____ Direction _____

Time Crossed Bar _____ Water Temp _____

Notes _____

_____

River/Bay Fishing

River Flow _____CFS Water Temp _____

Water Clarity _____ Drift or Motor Boat (circle)

Notes _____

_____

Crab Pots

Location/waypoints _____

Time In _____ Time Out _____

Pots _____ # Females _____

Males _____ # Keepers _____

Notes _____

_____

Time	Location	Depth	Species "K"eeper - "R"eleased	Length	Weight	Troll, Drift, Stationary	Bait/Lure

Date _____ Time Launch _____AM/PM Time Out _____AM/PM

Port/Dock _____

Fishing Buddies _____

High Tide_____ Low Tide _____

Sunrise _____AM Sunset _____PM

Air Temp Range _____ Barometric Pressure _____

Wind _____Kts Gusts _____Kt

Weather AM   Sunny / Pt Cloudy / Cloudy / Lt Rain / Rain / Heavy Rain

Weather PM   Sunny / Pt Cloudy / Cloudy / Lt Rain / Rain / Heavy Rain

Ocean Fishing

Wind Waves Ft/s _____ /_____ Direction _____

Swells Ft/s _____ / _____ Direction _____

Time Crossed Bar _____ Water Temp _____

Notes _____

_____

River/Bay Fishing

River Flow _____CFS Water Temp _____

Water Clarity _____ Drift or Motor Boat (circle)

Notes _____

_____

Crab Pots

Location/waypoints _____

Time In _____ Time Out _____

Pots _____ # Females _____

Males _____ # Keepers _____

Notes _____

_____

Time	Location	Depth	Species "K"eeper - "R"eleased	Length	Weight	Troll, Drift, Stationary	Bait/Lure

Date _____ Time Launch _____AM/PM Time Out _____AM/PM

Port/Dock _____

Fishing Buddies _____

High Tide_____ Low Tide _____

Sunrise _____AM Sunset _____PM

Air Temp Range _____ Barometric Pressure _____

Wind _____Kts Gusts _____Kts

Weather AM   Sunny / Pt Cloudy / Cloudy / Lt Rain / Rain / Heavy Rain

Weather PM   Sunny / Pt Cloudy / Cloudy / Lt Rain / Rain / Heavy Rain

Ocean Fishing

Wind Waves Ft/s _____ /_____ Direction _____

Swells Ft/s _____ / _____ Direction _____

Time Crossed Bar _____ Water Temp _____

Notes _____

_____

River/Bay Fishing

River Flow _____CFS Water Temp _____

Water Clarity _____ Drift or Motor Boat (circle)

Notes _____

_____

Crab Pots

Location/waypoints _____

Time In _____ Time Out _____

Pots _____ # Females _____

Males _____ # Keepers _____

Notes _____

_____

Time	Location	Depth	Species "K"eeper - "R"eleased	Length	Weight	Troll, Drift, Stationary	Bait/Lure

Date _____ Time Launch _____AM/PM Time Out _____AM/PM

Port/Dock _____

Fishing Buddies _____

High Tide_____ Low Tide _____

Sunrise _____AM Sunset _____PM

Air Temp Range _____ Barometric Pressure _____

Wind _____Kts Gusts _____Kts

Weather AM   Sunny / Pt Cloudy / Cloudy / Lt Rain / Rain / Heavy Rain

Weather PM   Sunny / Pt Cloudy / Cloudy / Lt Rain / Rain / Heavy Rain

Ocean Fishing

Wind Waves Ft/s _____ /_____ Direction _____

Swells Ft/s _____ / _____ Direction _____

Time Crossed Bar _____ Water Temp _____

Notes _____

_____

River/Bay Fishing

River Flow _____CFS Water Temp _____

Water Clarity _____ Drift or Motor Boat (circle)

Notes _____

_____

Crab Pots

Location/waypoints _____

Time In _____ Time Out _____

Pots _____ # Females _____

Males _____ # Keepers _____

Notes _____

_____

Time	Location	Depth	Species "K"eeper - "R"eleased	Length	Weight	Troll, Drift, Stationary	Bait/Lure

Date _____ Time Launch _____AM/PM Time Out _____AM/PM

Port/Dock _____

Fishing Buddies _____

High Tide_____ Low Tide _____

Sunrise _____AM Sunset _____PM

Air Temp Range _____ Barometric Pressure _____

Wind _____Kts Gusts _____Kts

Weather AM   Sunny / Pt Cloudy / Cloudy / Lt Rain / Rain / Heavy Rain

Weather PM   Sunny / Pt Cloudy / Cloudy / Lt Rain / Rain / Heavy Rain

Ocean Fishing

Wind Waves Ft/s _____ /_____ Direction _____

Swells Ft/s _____ / _____ Direction _____

Time Crossed Bar _____ Water Temp _____

Notes _____

_____

River/Bay Fishing

River Flow _____CFS Water Temp _____

Water Clarity _____ Drift or Motor Boat (circle)

Notes _____

_____

Crab Pots

Location/waypoints _____

Time In _____ Time Out _____

Pots _____ # Females _____

Males _____ # Keepers _____

Notes _____

_____

Time	Location	Depth	Species "K"eeper – "R"eleased	Length	Weight	Troll, Drift, Stationary	Bait/Lure

Made in the USA
Middletown, DE
08 April 2021